Hε

Dedication:
To my precious wife, Julie:
Thank your for your idea to create
this little book, and thank you for
editing and putting it together!

Also by Andrew Matthews:
  BEING HAPPY!
  MAKING FRIENDS
  GET FAXED!
  FOLLOW YOUR HEART.

Happiness in a Nutshell

Published by:
SEASHELL PUBLISHERS PTY LTD
PO Box 325, Trinity Beach
Queensland, AUSTRALIA, 4879
Fax 61 740 576 966
Website: www.seashell.com.au
E-mail:info@seashell.com.au

Layout and design by:
Seashell Publishers

First published October 1999
1st reprint November 1999
2nd reprint February 2000
3rd reprint July 2000
4th reprint April 2001
5th reprint January 2002
6th reprint March 2002
7th reprint August 2002
8th reprint February 2003
9th reprint April 2003
10th reprint June 2004

ISBN 0 9577572 6 3

Happiness
in a Nutshell

written and illustrated by
Andrew Matthews

Seashell Publishers
AUSTRALIA

Usually, the best place
to make a new start
is where you are!

Before changing your address,
consider changing your thinking!

When you change,
your situation changes.
It is law.

We all fail.

But it is not failing that hurts.
What hurts is knowing that
you didn't give your best.

Have the discipline to do
little things you don't like -

and you can spend your life
doing the big things you do like.

8

Happy people don't
just accept change,
they *embrace* it!

They are the people who say:
"Why would I want
my next five years
to be like my last five?"

The moment you get
too attached to things,
people, money ...
you screw it up!

The challenge of life
is to appreciate everything
and attach yourself
to nothing.

On giving advice:
If people aren't asking you,
they usually don't want
the information!

The first law of expansion is "order".
For something to grow, it needs system.

Look at a flower, cut an orange,
check out the symmetry
of a tree or a beehive.

There is discipline.

Nature keeps what is essential
and gets rid of the garbage.
It's called organisation.

You get motivated by *doing* things,
not thinking about them.

Next time you are upset,
remember it's not so much
people who make you angry,
as your thoughts about them.

Whatever thoughts
are causing you pain,
they are only thoughts.
You can change a thought.

The more emotional
you are about things,
the less control you have.

Most people are
very emotional about money -
so they are out of control.

Following your dream
is no guarantee of an easy ride.

Life usually becomes *more* challenging,
but you embark on an outer journey
which starts the inner journey.

You have a chance to blossom -
to see who you really are.

Where did we get the idea that
if we don't forgive people, *they* suffer?

For the world to treat you well,
you have to treat yourself well.

How can you feel
like a mover and shaker
when you have holes
in your underwear?

Every "disaster" in your life
is not so much a disaster,
as a situation waiting for you
to change your mind about it.

MATTHEWS

Most of us learned things inside out!

We learned:
*"If you don't like your job, change it.
If you don't like your wife, change her."*

Sometimes it's appropriate
to change your job or your partner.
But if you don't change too,
you are setting yourself up
for more of the same.

When we forgive ourselves,
we stop criticising other people.

Because we are always attracting
the learning experiences we need,
we often attract what we fear.

If you fear loneliness,
you'll attract that.
If you fear embarrassment,
you'll fall on your face.

It's life's way of encouraging us to grow.
The only way to beat fear is to face it.

When your *body* hurts, pain reminds you to take a rest, or maybe to change your shoes or to find a better way.

When your *mind* hurts, pain reminds you to quit worrying or to be more forgiving, or to think a different way.

Pain is not your enemy.
Pain is your friend!

26

Courage is not the absence of fear -
courage is acting in spite of fear.

People who do nothing
with their lives are just as scared
as people who take major risks.

It's just that the first group
get scared over tiny things.

Why not get scared
over something significant?

If we are honest with ourselves,
we can list almost everything
that's ever happened to us -
and see how we helped create it.

Start anywhere you can.

Give your best shot
to whatever is in front of you,
and opportunity will begin to find you.

It's called developing a reputation.

The happiest people
don't worry too much
about whether life is fair or not.
They just get on with it.

If you want
more peace of mind,
stop labeling
everything that happens
as "good" or "bad".

If you think the world
is against you, it is.
Blaming other people
doesn't work.

When you fight life,
life always wins.

The universe is always
nudging us with gentle signals.
When we miss the signals,
it nudges us with a
sledgehammer.

Growth is most painful
when we resist it.

If there is something
in your life you don't want,
stop worrying about it
and stop talking about it!

The energy you put into it
keeps it alive.
Withdraw your energy
and it will likely go away.

Your mission in life
is not to be
without problems -
your mission
is to get excited.

What you
focus on expands ...
so think about
what you want!

Detachment is a major reason
why rich people get richer.

They don't care so much -
they're not desperate.

There's a big difference
between a poor person's attitude -
wishing you had it -
and a wealthy person's approach -
believing you'll get it.

40

To see things differently,
you don't need willpower,
self confidence,
or brain surgery.
You just need the courage
to think the unfamiliar.

Your beliefs determine
your quality of life.

The balance
in your bank book
is not the measure
of your abundance.

Abundance is
what's circulating
through your life.

Your life will only work
when you take full responsibility
for your choices.

Your choice of vocation
is at the top of the list.

Nature seeks balance,
and you can't be
desperate and balanced.

Life doesn't have to be
an endless struggle.
Let things flow.

The universe has no favourites.
Your success and happiness
depend on natural laws and principles -
and how you use them.

Every event
has the potential
to transform us,
and disasters have
the greatest potential
to change our thinking.

Life happens in waves.
This means family crises,
wedding invitations and car repairs
tend to travel in bunches.

When you strike a month
without bills, you say to yourself:
*"I'll put something aside
for the next wave."*

When you get swamped by the
next wave, you say to yourself:
"This is only temporary".

We are not here
to be punished.

We are here
to be educated.

Simplify your life.
Quit doing things out of habit.
Eliminate some of the garbage
from your routine so you can see
your path more clearly.

Your life is
a perfect reflection
of your beliefs.

When you change
your deepest beliefs
about the world,
your life changes
accordingly.

Once we make a decision
to do a thing,
the means appear.
We might explain away
these lucky breaks
as coincidence.
But with keen observation,
we notice it happens regularly.

To succeed at anything,
you don't need to be a genius.
But you do need a good plan!

Most people quit!

Start every day
with an intention
to be balanced and peaceful.

Some days you will
cruise through until bedtime,
and some days you won't
make it past breakfast.

If peace of mind is your daily goal,
you will get better and better.

Your mission in life
is not to change the world.

Your mission is to change yourself.

There are no "outside" solutions,
only "inside" solutions.

You give your best
not because you need
to impress people.

You give your best because
that's the only way
to enjoy your work.

"Get off your butt and do something!"

The joy is in doing your thing -
and stretching because you choose to,
not because you have to.

Whatever you do for a living
is a vehicle to connect
with people.

Fred says:
*"I think like I do
because my life is a mess!"*
No Fred, your life is a mess
because you think
like you do!

62

We are here to learn lessons,
and the world is our teacher.

When we fail to learn a lesson,
we get to take it again ... and again!

Once we have learned the lesson,
we move on to the next one.

(And we never run out of lessons!)

God is never
going to come down
from a cloud and say:
*"You now have permission
to be successful!"*

You have to
give yourself
permission.

The question is always:
*"What are you doing
with what you have?"*

While the answer is *"not much"*,
nothing gets better.

The universe rewards effort,
not excuses.

The law of the seed:
effort + *patience* = results.
You reap your harvest
after you do the work.

Doing what you love
is not a recipe for an easier life.

It is a recipe for an interesting life.

If you don't know
what you like doing,
maybe you stopped listening
to yourself years ago.

Many of us became different people
in order to please everyone else.

When life is sweet,
and that little voice says:
"It can't last!" Tell yourself:
"Maybe it's about to get better!"

Life goes like this ...

We get hit by little pebbles -
as a kind of warning.

When we ignore the pebbles,
we get hit by a brick.
Ignore the brick and we get
wiped out by a boulder.

If we are honest, we can see
where we have ignored the warning signs.
And then we have the nerve to say:
"Why me?"

Peace of mind doesn't come
from having less problems -
it comes from being less critical!

Loving people means
giving them the freedom
to be who they choose to be
and where they choose to be.

Love is allowing people to be
in your life out of choice.

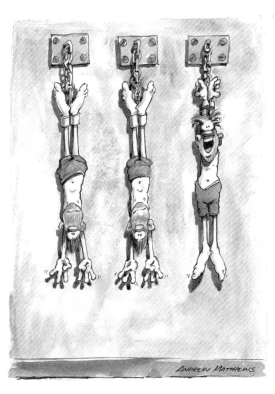

*"Sometimes I ask myself:
'Why am I the lucky one?'"*

When have you made
the most important decisions in your life?
When you were on your knees -
after disasters, after knock-backs,
when you've been kicked in the head.
That's when we say to ourselves:
"I'm sick of being broke,
sick of being kicked around.
I'm tired of being mediocre.
I'm going to do something."

We learn our biggest lessons
when things get rough.

In order to have something
in your life and keep it -
whether it's a job, or a relationship -
you have to be comfortable with it.

To make money and keep it,
you must be comfortable with money!

To find, you have to seek.

If you have lost your life direction,
you probably won't find it
between drinks at the local bar.

Give yourself a break,
give yourself some time and space
to examine what counts for you.

78

Act as if every event has a purpose,
and your life will have purpose.

Figure out why you needed
an experience, conquer it,
and you won't need it again.

Ultimately, you can only
depend on your inner guidance -
in other words,
follow your heart.

"FOLLOW YOUR HEART"

ISBN 0-646-31066-6
International #1 bestseller about:
- doing what you love
- how rich people think
- dealing with disasters
- finding purpose in your life and work.

"BEING HAPPY!"

ISBN 981-00-0664-0
Over 1 million copies sold in 18 languages.
It is about:
- forgiving yourself
- being able to laugh at yourself
- how happy people think
- the power of your thoughts!

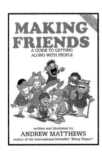

"MAKING FRIENDS"

ISBN 981-00-1953-X
International bestselling
guidebook about:
- relationships
- dealing with anger
- being able to say "no"
- enjoying people.